TODAY'S TOP DRIVERS

MARCUS ERICSSON

BY KATE MIKOLEY

Gareth Stevens Publishing

HOT TOPICS

Please visit our website, www.garethstevens.com. For a free color catalog of all our high-quality books, call toll free 1-800-542-2595 or fax 1-877-542-2596.

Library of Congress Cataloging-in-Publication Data
Names: Mikoley, Kate, author.
Title: Marcus Ericsson / Kate Mikoley.
Description: Buffalo, N.Y. : Gareth Stevens Publishing, [2024] | Series: Today's top drivers | Includes bibliographical references and index.
Identifiers: LCCN 2023012814 | ISBN 9781538287200 (library binding) | ISBN 9781538287194 (paperback) | ISBN 9781538287217 (ebook)
Subjects: LCSH: Ericsson, Marcus, 1990–Juvenile literature. | Automobile racing drivers–Sweden–Biography–Juvenile literature.
Classification: LCC GV1032.E75 M55 2024 | DDC 796.72092 [B]–dc23/eng/20230316
LC record available at https://lccn.loc.gov/2023012814

First Edition

Published in 2024 by
Gareth Stevens Publishing
2544 Clinton St
Buffalo, NY 14224

Designer: Tanya Dellaccio Keeney
Editor: Kate Mikoley

Photo credits: Series background Merydolla/Shutterstock.com; cover, pp. 5, 17, 19, 21, 23, 27, 29 Grindstone Media Group/Shutterstock.com; p. 7 https://upload.wikimedia.org/wikipedia/commons/5/5b/Marcus_Ericsson.JPG; p. 9 https://upload.wikimedia.org/wikipedia/commons/f/ff/Marcus_Ericsson_2009_Macau_F3.jpg; p. 11 Jordan Tan/Shutterstock.com; p. 13 ZRyzner/Shutterstock.com; pp. 15 (top), 25 PatrickLauzon photographe/Shutterstock.com; p. 15 (bottom) cristiano barni/Shutterstock.com.

Printed in the United States of America

CONTENTS

MEET MARCUS

When it comes to car racing, there's more than just one style, or kind. Some drivers don't stick to just one style of racing—they try a few! Marcus Ericsson is one of those drivers. Today, he's known for IndyCar racing, but that wasn't always the case.

IN THE FAST LANE

*IndyCar is a **series** of races in North America. The cars have one seat and open wheels.*

Ericsson was born September 2, 1990, in Sweden. He got his start in racing when he was just 9 years old. He started out driving a small kind of race car known as a kart or go-kart.

IN THE FAST LANE

Lots of race car drivers start out driving karts. It's a way for kids to get used to being behind the wheel.

FUN IN FORMULA

Formula is a kind of racing where the cars have one seat and open wheels. The place where the driver sits, called a cockpit, is also open. By 2007, Ericsson was driving in formula races. That year, he won the Formula BMW UK.

IN THE FAST LANE

In 2009, Ericsson won Japan's Formula 3 ***championship.***

The top class of formula racing is Formula 1 (F1). Before F1, many drivers spend time racing in Formula 2 (F2). F2 used to be called GP2. Ericsson started racing in the GP2 series in 2010. He took part in the series for four seasons.

IN THE FAST LANE

*Ericsson went up in the **rankings** each season he was in the GP2 series. In his final year in the series, 2013, he finished in sixth place.*

ON TO FORMULA 1

In 2014, Ericsson started driving in F1. He was racing for Caterham, a British car maker. The team was not doing well with money, so for the 2015 season, Ericsson agreed to drive for Sauber, a well-known team in **motorsports**.

IN THE FAST LANE

When Ericsson started racing in F1, he was the first driver from Sweden to do so in more than 20 years!

Ericsson continued racing in F1 until 2018. He held his own on the track, but never managed to break into the top five in a race. His best ranking came in his final year of F1, when he finished in 17th place.

IN THE FAST LANE

All kinds of car racing come with danger. In 2018, Ericsson was in a scary crash at practice. Luckily, he wasn't badly hurt.

GETTING INTO INDY

In 2019, Ericsson made the move to the IndyCar series. He raced for Schmidt-Peterson Motorsports and drove the No. 7 Honda. He got his first IndyCar podium when he came in second place in Detroit.

IN THE FAST LANE

The podium is where drivers get honored when they come in first, second, or third place. When a driver finishes in the top three, it's known as "a podium."

In 2021, Ericsson got his first two IndyCar wins. These were in Belle Isle and Nashville. He had 10 more top-10 finishes that season. This led to him finishing in sixth place.

IN THE FAST LANE

Ericsson was tied for second-most top-10 finishes in 2021.

A WIN AT INDY

If fans thought Ericsson's 2021 season was good, they were blown away by his 2022 results. While he only had one win that year, it was at the biggest race of them all: the Indianapolis 500! Two more podiums helped him land sixth place for the season.

IN THE FAST LANE

IndyCar is named after the Indianapolis 500. It's the most well-known race in the sport!

Winning an Indy 500 is perhaps the best way to put an IndyCar driver on the map. Hundreds of thousands of people go to the race, and millions more watch on television. Ericsson was the second person from Sweden to ever win the race.

IN THE FAST LANE

Ericsson was the 27th Indy 500 winner to have also raced in F1.

OFF THE TRACK

Before he was a race car driver, Ericsson played another sport. As a kid, he played hockey. He still enjoys watching hockey. He also likes staying in touch with fans by posting often on his **social media** pages.

IN THE FAST LANE

When watching hockey, Ericsson roots for, or backs, the Swedish national team.

DRIVING FORWARD

As of 2023, Ericsson drives for Chip Ganassi Racing and Huski Chocolate. He has more than a dozen top-five finishes in IndyCar to his name, and chances are there are more yet to come.

IN THE FAST LANE

Chip Ganassi has been a well-known racing team for as long as Ericsson has been alive! Together, the team's members have won more than 200 races.

Ericsson started the 2023 season off by winning the **Grand Prix** of St. Petersburg. He wasn't winning for most of the race, but took the lead in lap 97 out of 100. His ability to pull ahead to win is just one **quality** that makes him a great driver!

IN THE FAST LANE

Ericsson won the Grand Prix of St. Petersburg by 2.4 seconds. That may not seem like much, but in a sport where it often comes down to less than a second, that's a pretty strong win!

TIMELINE

SEPTEMBER 2, 1990

ERICSSON IS BORN.

2007

HE WINS THE FORMULA BMW UK.

2009

ERICSSON WINS THE JAPAN FORMULA 3 CHAMPIONSHIP.

2010

HE STARTS RACING IN THE GP2 SERIES.

2014

HE STARTS DRIVING IN F1.

2019

ERICSSON STARTS RACING IN INDYCAR.

2022

HE WINS THE INDY 500.

FOR MORE INFORMATION

BOOKS

Braulick, Carrie A. *Indy Cars*. North Mankato, MN: Capstone Press, 2019.

Mikoley, Kate. *The Indianapolis 500*. New York, NY: Gareth Stevens Publishing, 2021.

Rule, Heather. *GOATs of Auto Racing*. Minneapolis, MN: SportsZone, 2022.

WEBSITES

Marcus Ericsson
www.chipganassiracing.com/drivers/mericsson
Read a short bio of Ericsson here.

Marcus Ericsson
www.espn.com/racing/driver/_/id/4622/marcus-ericsson
Find the latest race results on Ericsson's ESPN driver's page.

Marcus Ericsson
www.indycar.com/Series/IndyCar-Series/Marcus-Ericsson
Find Ericsson's latest stats on the IndyCar website.

GLOSSARY

championship: A contest to decide an overall winner.

grand prix: One of a series of international car races.

motorsport: A type of sport that involves racing vehicles with motors.

quality: A feature, often one that shows someone's character or abilities.

ranking: The position or order a person is in within a group.

series: A set of events or races that go together.

social media: Websites and other forms of online communication where users share information.

INDEX